Steeling Effects

Jane Byers

CAITLIN PRESS

01 02 03 04 05 06 19 18 17 16 15 14

Caitlin Press Inc.
8100 Alderwood Road,
Halfmoon Bay, BC V0N 1Y1
www.caitlin-press.com

Text design by Kathleen Fraser.
Cover design by Vici Johnstone.
Cover photo copyright Vici Johnstone.
Printed in Canada.

Caitlin Press Inc. acknowledges financial support from the Government of Canada through the Canada Book Fund and the Canada Council for the Arts, and from the Province of British Columbia through the British Columbia Arts Council and the Book Publisher's Tax Credit.

 Canada Council   Conseil des Arts
for the Arts   du Canada

 BRITISH COLUMBIA
ARTS COUNCIL
An agency of the Province of British Columbia

Library and Archives Canada Cataloguing in Publication
Byers, Jane, 1966–, author
    Steeling effects / Jane Byers.

Poems.
ISBN 978-1-927575-44-4 (bound)

    I. Title.

PS8603.Y47S74 2014   C811'.6   C2013-908451-7

Steeling Effects

To Amy Bohigian and our children, Frances and Theodore.

CONTENTS

Sac

STILL

We are rushed to surgery on a tippling gurney
taut skin sliced clean through
to the bulging womb.

The pink sacs of my newborn lungs turn deep blue,
not the azure of the sky
but the darkening blue of alarm.

SOLO JOURNEY I

Unswayed by anoxia,
my lungs wait.

My skin sinks and deepens to navy,
oblivious to the doctor's attempts,
and my mother's distress.
At long last, it is I who choose to breathe.

I have a self.

A bundle of will,
no explanation but corpuscular belief,
placenta-rich wisdom,
oracular newborn.

MEMBRANE

I must have grown accustomed
to the alone of the isolette.
Starched nurses march their rounds,
flick my feet when I forget to breathe.

Tube-fed, temperature-regulated,
ventilated: every vital sign monitored
in that illuminated box.
I mimic the vigilance of machines;
still, I choose to breathe.

The sacs' resilience stuns:
semi-permeable,
        they empty and fill,
making a case for faith.

SOLO JOURNEY II

As a newborn, I was complicit only in being alive.

At nine, separation from self,
while my body endures crushing assault,
depleted of oxygen with the blunt force of him.

During the rape, I split in two—
one part examines the red velvet crowns
on the bedroom walls of a friend's house
while another thinks about the creamsicle of my family's
orange carport and white shag rug.

All of my cells recall the blue alarm of birth.
I try to will myself impermeable,
as my own sacs deform
with the question of blame—
the slip into complicity,
galloping consumption.
Still, complicity carries a delusion of power,
keeps me from complete collapse.

ENDURANCE

My soul braces—
    builds me an iron lung
    from shards of my birth experience,
    to keep me intact.
Artificial respiration
until alveoli remember and
my study of cells commences.

Membranes have a high tolerance for deformation.

Yet, it's more years in a kind of isolette,
nothing cracked.
It will be a decade before I seek a healer
who can hold and cajole
me
into exhaling stale air,
until my body consents to soften,
to breathe again on its own.

WHAT DOESN'T KILL YOU…

My first journey alone from uterus to incubator,
an inoculation against despair.

I study resilience.
I search for cracks in structures
returned to their original shape
after assault.

Breakwaters eventually break.

I vow to mimic the tensile strength of a spider web
and the mutability of bacteria
that render them resilient,

not the succor of cement.

I breathe my way back,

empty and fill,

to belief in my pliant self.

Lonely, No, Not Lonely

With their modest football pool winnings Blanche and Joe could have
bought their dank row house that fronted the cotton mill,
but she insisted, instead, on a motorbike and side car—
the first conveyance on their street.
All four of them puttered round the continent,
canvas tent, cold chips and a flask of tea stuffed between children's feet.

A respite from the grey of Northern England,
her kerchief tight round her chin,
held high in defiance of the lashing rain,
as they laboured towards the south of France;
all the rest of the town trudged forty miles on bus and train
to the scrappy seaside for their annual holiday
near the cheap promenade and the frigid sea.

Their neighbours Joyce, Aubrey, Cyril and Fanny gather on Central Pier.
Who does she think she is then? Were it her given name, Blanche?
Is it French? Her mummy putting on airs. It weren't France
that won the war though were it? Our lads liberated them.
Besides, the Third Reich ain't far once you wind up
on that ferry to Calais. They'd rather bed down with
Krauts than with their own kind on English soil.

There, there, luv, nought wrong with us. Let's go
to the Pleasure Beach. Let's find us some toffee
and a pint. We'll 'ave a smashing time.

Gallivanting over God's green earth. Those little ones stuffed
in that sidecar. I've heard she calls herself Bianca in Spain.

The illuminations are first rate, we'll stroll on the promenade.
Could've bought the 2-up 2-down with their winnings. You'll
see, pet, in thirty years, who owns their own home,
and how that motorbike runs.

The Byers family disembarks the Triumph
as neighbours wave their pasty hands
and sallow children with the last bites of Blackpool rock in their mouths
gather round the sidecar at the end of July holidays.
Joe tanned under a beret and Blanche with a new headscarf,
the children with their madeleines.

Blanche says, "In the south of France, the fabric on the lines was so pretty."
Mmmm, yeah. Well, here, grey matches the
factory, and besides it's only clothes.

When the house is asleep, she push-pins the postcards
into the cold wall behind the sideboard:
Côte d'Azur, Madrid, Dutch fields.
Most nights she faces them, her back to the gas fire.

Neighbours tut at her pauper's wake
while quaffing cheap sherry and store-bought biscuits,
as they peer into her pine box,
lined with faded postcards of wildflowers
on hillsides and Athenian ruins.

INAUGURAL FLIGHT

By invitation of the pretty British Airways stewardess,
I walked the aisle west to the complicated cockpit.
What held my attention was not the instruments or their operators
but the sky beyond the windshield,
more depth than I could fathom
and a horizon larger than the pea-green boat or
the owl and the pussycat ever sailed towards.
It was just the vastness and me.

I knew my life was somewhere out there
beyond the constant horizon and not in
the slim seats my parents occupied, anticipating a meal.
Nor in the joystick or flicked switch of the pilot.
Beyond even my new country, Ca-na-da.
Even its land mass could not contain my gaze,
not unlike the blue ceiling my newborn eyes scanned
through the incubator for six days.

Lonely, no, not lonely,
profoundly alone, always
the deepest times in my life alone.

BASEBALL

My parents bought me a left-hand glove,
because I am left-handed.
They did their best,
parsing the mystery of foreign gestures:
the coach touching his peaked cap, tapping his chest,
the crouched catcher signalling between his legs.
They asked what kind of sport was played on a diamond;
was the soil hard? Would I be rich?
And home plate—was it made of china?
Why is the shortstop not short? What is a bullpen?
Some days I answered patiently.

Another glove was out of the question.
I knew not to ask,
savings gone,
less meat for a week
because of a leather extravagance.
"Cricket players don't wear gloves"
was quickly shushed by my mother.

After weeks of quiet practice,
I learned to throw with my right hand.
Pitched tennis balls careened off the garage wall,
never accurate, but I did get stronger.

Peering from left field, I hoped for pop flies
but other things distracted me,
like the way they sat erect in the stands,
reading their foreign paper. My teammates
would squint at the outfield following

the line drive to my outstretched glove.
Their cheers prompted my parents' mistimed applause
as I hurled the ball in an errant direction.

I gripped the bat and swatted like mad at the incoming pitch
but half of swing is attitude.
I tried to earn my way with a solid hit,
then, stranded on base, I waited for the coach's signal,
though stealing home is always tougher than it looks.

Baseball is not a game of effort so much as belonging,
each fielder standing alone, occupying territory
or planted over home plate, guarding inheritance.

POND HOCKEY

Summer's cesspool transformed into an oblong
ice rink on the limestone-sculpted landscape,
across the farmer's field from our house.
We'd take the surface as we found it,
always hope for no snow, for smoothness,
but cracked or bumpy
the boys in a one-mile radius and I
played hockey for hours
after shovelling it clear to its dark nuance.

I'd sit on my butt to put on my figure skates
as the damp cold soaked through my clothes.
The meagre heat of that distant sun
no match for the Ontario wind chill.
The icy puck against my snow pants, thin protection
as I stickhandled like Sittler, in my glory,
to the goalposts of frozen boots.

The youngest kid was decreed goalie,
usually my little brother, who hated hockey.
I took slapshots at his toque-clad head until my arms ached
then I let him skate, but I soon longed
for the screech and scrape of my blades,
and there are no referees meting out justice,
so he was promptly back in net.

I was always the last one, begging for the boys to stay:
as dusk fell I careened past the others to score once more,
I lingered in the smell of sweaty hockey gloves
the rich kids wore, while my brother
gunned for the front door.

The pond hasn't frozen over in years.
A thin film of ice sometimes threatens,
but thaws on those frequent slushy days
and the kids go to the arena to play,
segregated by sex and age,
on artificial ice.

The cow pond is still there,
though unbelievably small.
The farm still exists on the difficult land—
the rock quarry, the grazing grass for heifers
and farmer Hunt, if he's alive, is an old man.

ADVANCE PENANCE FOR A MALADJUSTED SON

My mom slows the royal blue Buick round the big bend
to a halt, a mile from home,
ten steps past the woman thumbing it with her kids.
Mom tells her to get in.

Her cracked leather jacket squeaks in the cold.
Her youngest son piles in the front;
her eldest, with his fringed suede coat, has to sit with my brothers and
    me in the back.
"Where you going?"
"Millhaven."
"We aren't going that far. Do you live there?"
"Their dad does."
"I'll drive you."

Both mothers smoke, then mine asks, "Where can I drop you off?"
"Anywhere here," but my mom wants to drive her to the door.
"Okay. Left here, right here."
"The penitentiary?

We pull up to the guardhouse;
rolls of barbed wire spiral over the concrete walls.
The man in the turret has a gun.
My mom says, "I hope it goes well."
"Thanks for the ride," as she gathers her plastic bag and kids.

The quiet car smells of cold leather and cigarette smoke.
I finally ask, "Why are people in jail?"
"For stealing," she says too quickly.

I glance at my brother.
His blonde hair and blue eyes do not betray his guilt.
Stealing jujubes and penny candies from the drunken shopkeeper,
and selling them at school for a healthy profit—
he's still somewhere between a crook and a capitalist.

TEENAGERS TALK ABOUT SEX

I'm drawn to and dread the slumber party chatter:
When was your first experience?
Have you kissed a boy, gone to second base?
Sometimes I say nothing,
because baseball is not an apt euphemism.
Other times I brag, "I had sex already," and
my thirteen-year-old friends all stop and stare.
The healthy ones cringe,
then I say, "Joking," instead of mentioning choking.
Even so they know there's something wrong,
I'm telling them my story framed in false consent.
Most of the time, even now, I keep quiet about sex,
when it started for me and what came after.

It was moat dark.
The drifts crenellated across the sports field,
deep and white.
I ran and fell, ran and fell,
slipping into varying depths of snow, on ice, alone,
penetrating the crust.

I couldn't outrun him.
He'd finally caught up,
twelve years later
on this college campus miles from home,
and scalded me with violent memories.
The drifts muffled my voice.
As the sear melted the snow,
it pooled around me,
the wet, miserable truth.
At least I could feel the puddle,
however unpleasant. I knew
a dark river of thaw.

When I could cry no more,
I limped back to my dorm.
There were no turrets in the dorm's concrete walls.
After a hot bath, I entered the green of my room,
tucked myself naked in the calm sheets.
For the first time I noticed their touch,
real and smooth.
Their weight did not hurt.

RAPE, NOT LACROSSE

One in fifty play lacrosse.
In our town, it was more like one in three.
I knew a player once, clad in pride and an orange jersey.
His gym bag smelled like any other teenage boy's.
His stick leaned against the railing to the upstairs bedrooms,
its smooth shaft dark from gripping.
He wielded the stick but followed no rules,
rammed it inside me, split my nine-year-old self in two.

I wonder if he still plays
or if his cudgel is hung by its cat gut
from a dark hook
in his parents' house.
For all I know it leans in the entrance
of his own home,
in his wife's and anyone else's plain view.

I walk past a lacrosse game in progress.
In my mind, I pinch a stick from the players' bench.
Its thickness startles me,
so I burn it for warmth,
take pictures for the Minister of Sport.
I suggest a change in funding
to something more widespread.
One in three women is raped—
a new national sport.

Most sessions something shifted.
Some days it shattered what I thought was bone
but turned out to be an ancient knot in soft tissue.
Weekly treatments mount;
I've slowly grown a new self.

Once a year I go alone;
this restaurant a respite from shame,
the family who runs it kind.
I sit at a plain table eating a sandwich,
pork pulled from ribs.
After all this rebuilding I am hungry.
I dip each bite into sauce.
The Portuguese bread absorbs juice—
I suck on its sustenance
and notice new curtains and candlelight.

The work of rebuilding, invisible to most.
The dense meat fills my belly,
its slow smoke sweet.
I dab the meal's remnants from the edges of my mouth.
They say bones can strengthen after a break.

Back out in the lit-up night, I squint
against false illuminations.
Metal wheels whine on tracks.
I ascend the tram's steps and
sit on a red bench.
The weight of protein outlasts sorrow.
The streetcar crawls forward.

GRISTLE

You know those tenacious bits embedded in the muscle of meat,
random clumps of fatty tissue that even your fangs can't tear through,
your saliva doesn't have a chance of breaking down.
Passed on from the cow's ancestors, these fragments persist,
a reminder the beasts have not entirely succumbed to slaughter.

Jawed out, your own taut muscles stop their ruminating,
your tongue and lips roll it around,
evading its edges, like a splinter in your mouth,
expel it into a napkin with a gob of inert spit.
Who wants a reminder of that indivisible past?
Of the tentacled mass, lodged in your chest
in response to some unspeakable loss.
Later you marvel when your gut-churning stops
and revere a grazing Holstein.

SQUALL

What started as a hurricane
has been downgraded to a tropical storm
off the coast of us.
These chronic small batterings
underlie our existence.
This time the big one didn't come.
Bittersweet relief as the storm moves on.
An exhausted new dawn takes its place.
But these unnamed gales accumulate.

In the harbour, the exfoliated hull of a battered dory
sways toward an uncertain future and
only the barnacles hold firm on the government pier.
Straked planks would have weathered this intact,
long, continuous commitments of wood,
but the builder chose other stock.

Unmoored we drift;
survival is an inadequate habit.
The deep sea
offers a glimmer of hope,
poison and antidote.
We jettison our faith, wish ourselves small—
ancient crustaceans—
yearn to fix ourselves
to something more permanent,
a breakwater to attenuate the storms.

INTENSIVE CARE

Yesterday's platinum injection offers protection
from the artery ballooning at the base of your brain.
Still, damage is done:
a chaos of blood uncontained,
your motherly eyes stray.

The nurse, a whir,
changes IVs, leans down,
checks the yellow catheter.
She dispenses relief
for your invaded cranium,
jots on your chart
and nods in our general direction.

You remember to smile and be gracious,
but forget your name.
Recognition spreads across your face
as you look at the rainbow rings
that have escaped the collar of the nurse's uniform.
"So, you're a lesbian," you say, clear as day.
The nurse pauses, rechecks fluid levels, the catheter—
hesitates, cautious as truth colours this dingy room.

Before the reply, your shaky arm points.
"It's okay, my daughter is too."
So relieved to hear you remember,
I forget my shame; begin to shed restraint.
As hope pools in the base of my brain,
we slip into intensive recovery.

STARFRUIT

Grandma saved me from Mum and Dad's green grocery shop,
where I played among the root vegetables
and my parents' distracted love,
as they served shoppers, arranged stock
and haggled with threadbare customers.

Grandma let me sit in the front seat of her Morris Minor.
Through the windshield, the treeless green of Lancashire hills,
on our way to endless cups of tea so Blanche could brag about me.
Azure sea of a postcard from Crete on her dash.
A Christmas star dangled from her mirror.
With her I knew one day I'd be as bright.

Mashed potatoes and turnip are nutrient-poor from the endless boil
but love doesn't leach.
I buy starfruit when I can.
Thin cross-sections make a constellation
atop my roasted salad of parsnips and beets.
They still dazzle me,
though I've learned it's roots that sustain.

Joy's Urgent Threshold

I never understood the deal
struck between the immortal twin and his father.
Pollux gives half his immortality to restore his mortal brother, Castor.
They both live forever. So what if they divide
their time between Mount Olympus and the underworld?
We still get half of every year with Gemini in the night sky.

Facing these empty cribs, I'd consider six months dwelling with Hades
for the gift of twins.
One hundred and eighty-two days with small hands in mine.

If the underworld is utter darkness and doubt, I'm already there.

As I labour up the midnight trail,
I imagine the shattering dark beneath,
but gazing up, I can't ignore ·
Venus and the vast constellations that light my way.
I stumble to the summit; it's a clear view but lonely.
Still, I'm considering the bargain, until
rising up over the mountains Mawu, the moon,
the female twin of Liza, appears.
This goddess of the night/motherhood won't let go.
Her moonlight shines on my bloodied feet.
I understand now that it's all or nothing.
I walk down the mountain in Castor's shoes.

AND WE HAVE HAD JULY WITH OUR BABY GIRL,
FOR THAT WE ARE THANKFUL
(from a friend's blog about the last days of their child's life)

Rainless July.

Blue sky for most people.
Dust chokes every trail.
Leukocytes accumulate
despite fierce drugs,
prayers,
her parents' tears,
her brother's desperate hugs.

Last night, in the waning minutes of July, there was a light rain.
At best it gives the garden another day
before romaine goes brittle and spinach bolts.
Reprieve.

LIFE DRAWING
On joy's urgent threshold, the door is held ajar[1]

The artist draws dead babies,
delicate loss, beauty in accuracy.
Still, I want her to draw my twins who live,
so I may understand the origin of their wills.

In the first snapshot they lie side by side,
on their faces no disdain,
their bodies perfect and small—
preemies.
Would her pencil lines stray to feeding tube,
heart monitor,
stump of umbilicus?
Could hatching convey them in their joint orbit—
private sphere of belonging?

They hover between worlds,
the door held ajar for thirty days by a resolute team:
nurses, social workers, even the birth mother,
eventually their foster mom.

Thirteen months until we found the fixed gaze of their cacao eyes.
A couple searching. Babies who didn't yet know they were waiting.
Joy postponed.

---

[1]   From "Undiagnosed" (*The Word for Sand*, Wolsak and Wynn, 1988) by
Heather Spears.

SWADDLED HANDS

He sleeps in his car seat,
shoes doffed, naked feet,
socks on his hands.
Would pass for whimsy
had we not known
that his first month was incubated
and alone.

Newborn mitts, thumbless,
so he wouldn't pull out the tubes.
His swaddled hands.
His birth mom laughed at the socks.
He has an easy laugh too
and then days when he sobs long and deep.

He dons socks still,
when the world is too much.
Toddler fingers bunched and warm,
soothed in an
exoskeleton of soft cotton.
He pretends it's a joke.

Beyond the drone of familiar words,
under the buffer of the story,
sadness floods her heart.
Ink streams
from an old fountain pen with its tip busted off,
willed to her by her mother.
The medical diagram
would show blue inhabiting her arteries,
obedient heart pumping the thick ink,
until her body appeared as a tattoo
of its inner self.

Like a squid in self-defense,
she releases a pool of ink—
covers a stretched canvas
until it is twilight blue.
Beneath it, she's written
Mother, I am not you.

Mottled rainbows on their faces,
her children bring watercolours—
a yellow, a red—
as they toddle towards her.

STORM WATCH

My daughter ducks under the throw
beside me on the couch;
my son waits, tiptoe on a chair,
wide-eyed stare across the lake.
The boom comes, the windowpanes shake,
he, too, rushes to burrow his head in me.
I count diminishing seconds from the lightning strike,
tell myself I'm not afraid.
"You're safe in the house," I say.
"Safe house," they yell, and run a small circle on the rug,
a frantic return with the next crack.

On the news, a massive mudslide,
houses plunder down a mountain,
splintered walls collapse trestles.
My kids are asleep and I feel grateful.

For now our house is safe,
granite foundation,
on the side of a mountain.
The twins will soon run a wide arc in the world.
I need some dry runs before the deluge,
to give them good odds and rubber boots.
With each thunderstorm, resilience.
I hope.

BIRTHRIGHT

Sometimes when you are crying,
I assume it's the usual toddler dissonance:
this difficult world too big to absorb.
Other times it is your primal loss,
that deep grief of absence—
a birth mother who was saying goodbye as she said hello,
a set of caregivers to bond to temporarily,
then us, your new parents.

Love is the whole journey.

Still, how to explain those essential people disappearing?
What's left is the efflorescence of tears on your face.
I hold you, you cry some more.
Now you insist, "I cry, I cry,"
as if it is your only birthright.
That lonely sob, a consent to loss.

My daughter is wailing again about what is not here.
Not her other mama, presently at work,
not her nana who raised her for the first year,
not her blue car in the drive (see mama, above).

If she knew that olive trees don't grow here, she'd mourn them too.
Or tsetse flies, or oranges—
she's predisposed.

At a loss while she sobs, I'm reading her a book before nap.
It's called *Lost and Found*:
a boy finds a penguin,
tries to repatriate it to the South Pole,
the penguin stands forlorn on the ice
as the boy rows away in his boat.
My daughter says, "Sometimes you leave me at the South Pole and
that makes me sad."

I row through our tears,
vowing to keep her close.
Where have I left her?
Like a politician, I blame the previous administration.
The boy returns for the penguin;
eventually, they find each other and go home.

Alone, in a quiet dawn, I scan the horizon for any truth.
The gap left in the birth mother's wake is a kind of truth
but so, too, is this—
primal loss repels primal loss.
I must re-examine my own southern jaunt.
Left adrift, I, too, know despair.
We must make our way back north
to that tropic of love.

Jutting into the river, a fluvial beach,
but before we rest on the picnic blanket,
we must ford a frigid torrent.
We choose a narrowish crossing that isn't too deep,
pants rolled up to our knees,
each of us carrying a twin,
some snacks, our shoes.
The smooth boulders taunt
the unaccustomed soles of our feet.
Murderous, aching-bone cold,
it occurs I'd do anything for the throbbing to stop,
though it's only a few moments and just knee deep.
I slip, then right myself while clutching my child.
Agony subsides; I release him onto the bank.
The four of us lie
on the pebbly blanket in the partial sun,
the toddlers poke cracker bits into our mouths,
throw branches at the current,
fall onto us for shelter from the valley's rare wind
until they topple off in a heap of giggles.

Soon the twins will tramp alone on the dry bed of the ephemeral creek,
but not before we wade back with them in our arms.

NO MOON
To Maya

She searches up through the night sky,
cries, "No moon, no moon."
Lips quivering, she argues
with its absence, makes a tiny fist,
howls with new-found abandon,
as I catch my breath
and hold fast to nothing.

How to say, "Sometimes there is no moon
and life's not fair."
Instead I mention the sun:
its daytime presence makes up for the moon gone,
but a toddler is unconsoled by tomorrow.
The moon is not there.
And even we must call it new.

Her eyes find another light.
"Baby moon, Mommy, baby moon,"
and all is right. Baby, how to tell you
it's more substantial than that.
Soon she will feel its tiny gravity, a child's tug,
as she gazes past the moon to other galaxies.

Tonight I spare her an empty explanation,
but know on a cloudy night soon,
she will stomp off betrayed.

RED IS THE COLOUR OF SPRING

Bloodshot eyes of new mothers testify,
nuances of green only a suspicion
of the faithful who believe in spring,
even forsythia are budless.
Still, my children shun their parkas,
insist on vinyl shells
too ventilated to resist chill.

He sports a firefighter slicker,
she a ladybug:
both shiny red with matching boots.
They command glances from each passerby,
stand firm on their diminishing snowmen,
with the arterial-blood holly-berry eyes.

I test my theory about red elsewhere, children in tow:
I bicycle to the low black river,
controlled by a dam, shallowest in spring.
Slippery river rocks refuse my feet.
I'm encouraged to walk above the high-water line
as if it's the rocks' right to peace;
the dogwoods' trumpet, still autumnal, screams *look at me.*

Puckered rosehips cling to old wood.
Rain dribbles from last year's dead apples,
rotted on the branches—
sludgy blood in need of oxygen
returns through hypoxic March
to spring's arterial flow.
My children blaze across ashen woods.

Each month, we take our twins to sit in the gym
with the other kids of colour in town.
Our children do their own thing in the corner while older kids skip
or flip wiffle balls with floor hockey sticks. Sometimes my son is clingy.
We mingle with the earnest white parents, celebrate Kwanzaa and Eid
with African food they spend hours preparing.
We bring store-bought cookies,
the kind with lots of butter and sugar and no ethnic tie.
Each time we mourn the loss of a Saturday skiing afternoon.

*

Long ago on an evening stroll down Commercial Street, Provincetown,
I enjoyed the gorgeous boys, scantily clad,
but it's the women holding hands that still get me.
All shapes, all ages, many would pass for Playboy-Bunny straight,
others welders and congresswomen.
This stirs the thrill I felt my first time there—
wide-eyed baby dyke seeing others like me.
No longer alone, something released—a soft red key.

*

My daughter has been asking why her eyes aren't blue,
why her skin is darker than mine.
Today, I'm not up for a genetics lesson with a three-year-old.
Instead, we trudge through slush to that monthly meeting.
This time we bring an Indian feast: *masala dosa, kulfi.*

I HOPE MY DAUGHTER DOESN'T STUDY ENTOMOLOGY

My five-year-old tugs my arm towards the frog pond at the four-star resort:
"Look, Mommy, those frogs are hugging, they must be best friends."

I am thankful her first brush with reproduction isn't the bedbug.

Relieved when I look under the memory-foam mattresses after check-in
that there aren't any signs of *Cimex lectularius*.
The male impales his bedbug mate in the abdomen
with a needle-like penis—
traumatic insemination, they call it.

The frogs float close and still.
It doesn't appear that the female is traumatized
or trying to escape.

SWEETNESS

My children craved sweets when they first came home.
I judged the foster mom for the candy she doled out
to fourteen-month-olds.

Four years in and I read about attachment post-adoption,
how, mimicking a newborn, children crave sweets,
yearn for connection with their new parents
as they would have yearned for their mother's milk.

Redoing their beginnings,
these brilliant beings,
who'd yet to say a word,
who'd smash each other with rattles,
careen in soggy diapers.

I cursed the sweets.
Withheld them,
fed the kids irritation instead.

Dessert now deep pleasure.

THANKSGIVING

First kindergarten projects posted in the hallways:
"I'm thankful for…"
My cat, my dog, my moms.

We don't have a cat.

She will learn what a political act the truth is;
she may be shushed or pitied or laughed at.

May she stretch out on the sill,
soaking in the sun, oblivious.

After four bowls of cereal, he makes a beeline,
stops at my feet, rockets his arms up,
all forty pounds of him gazing at me.
I peruse headlines:
the news as distant as the pea for the princess.
Email squawk.
My fingers stop their keyboard clack,
abandon the split second of busy protest,
the mounting dishes,
the assembly line of lunches.

I pick him up, walk to the couch,
his whole body against me—
warm clay.
Head burrowed in my neck,
his freshly-bathed-boy smell,
arms draped.
There is nothing else.
What is busy,
what is a day.

Entitlement Decisions

CHOP THE DAY

*"Damn the wretch who first set a sundial in the marketplace
and chopped my day into pieces."*

Plautus, playwright, 2 BC

Meticulous science
subdividing time into billionth segments.
Beyond our conscience,
atomic clocks split seconds so accurately
cesium atoms give in,
form an erratic picket line in time
protesting monotony and a meaningless pace.

The cathedral clock
still winds up, stands stoic and knowing.
Chronos, our stone-carved, obedient servant,
drags his old man's feet
to the weathered bell,
strikes noon or thereabouts
as trumpeting angels celebrate.
A few hours a century,
a donation to enduring beauty.

Temporal millionaires
amble to their daily reunion,
gather in the village square,
notice the sun's rays stretch languid
along the cobblestone lanes,
hear the clock strike.
They reject the progress
of grimy-jawed punch clocks,
of digital watches cuffed
to wrists, of alarm clocks.
All distant, unwelcome cousins
that fragment our days—
the old man would turn over
in his grave
at irregular intervals.

LADY ICARUS

I believe Icarus was not failing as he fell, but just coming to the end of his triumph.

Jack Gilbert

I would have joined the fire department
but it would be like continuing
a childhood fight
with my oldest brother
at the kitchen sink—him saying
it's a woman's job to wash dishes
as he sprawled his shortish legs on the counter,
watching pots drip dry, not lifting a finger.

The firemen loll about like superheroes
in the off-hours, leave the dishes in the sink
for when the "girls" come on shift.
They stuff the firewomen's lockers with hardcore porn
and command the junior women into the flames,
dragging uncharged hose until
they tumble like Icarus with melted wings.

The fervent start the fire
but their brothers stand by
until what's left is chaos and cinders
and a funeral pyre for tolerance.

DROP SHOT

i.

Firemen fret that a woman's
upper body strength is not enough to pull
their fallen from burning buildings.

To illustrate the point, the captain said,
"It took six of us struggling to get a fallen brother out."

Six.

Until they realized his jacket was hooked on something.
Perhaps a woman would have assessed the scene more closely,
relied less on brute strength.

ii.

Recovering from pneumonia in Grade Ten,
after no activity for eight weeks,
I needed to redefine my badminton game.
I walloped a taller, stronger boy
using the gentle drop shot—
precision, not force.
A slow-motion flop just across the net
had the gangly boy lunging and cursing
more than a smash ever could,
splintered his racquet
as he stormed off the court.

COMING OUT

They made me fire-hall pasta with ground beef
and spicy sausages,
more meat per square inch
than a slaughterhouse.
Four a.m. stomach revolt:
the meat, or adrenaline coursing at the chirpy alarms,
burning holes in my sleep
as I studied their job demands on the nightshift.

The firemen are polite, as if
cadet training includes how to treat the ladies.
When "woman in the hall" is blared over the PA,
they're all chivalry and smiles,
business as usual—
donning their bunker suits for an incident.

As I cut jicama and tempeh
into matchsticks for a salad,
I wonder what the boys at the hall would think.
I have to hope that some of them would like it.
On shift, I never came out as a vegetarian.

TO A POLITICIAN

The platoon chief sliced the structural gloves ragged
to approximate the firemen's lacerated palms,
so their compo claims would be accepted.
And then there's the falling-asleep-
at-the-wheel-of-a-fire-truck claims
due to second jobs as renovators and movie extras,
or just plain tired from fire-hall banter and early-morning
false alarms set off by cockroaches in housing projects,
or sprawling commutes or the tedium of nothing burning.

You've underestimated the brotherhood.
This is not the fraud you'd anticipated
when you promised an overhaul of the system.
You must keep your promise to slash and burn.
You've decided to go after welfare mothers instead.

I catch the elevator with the crew-cut chief and his assistants.
He says to the safety guy, "I hear you got divorced.
You a fag now?"
The slow elevator ascends four floors.
"Nah, nothing like that," he makes plain.
"Good, you've got a few girls then," the fire chief concludes
as the doors slide open.
Why didn't I take the stairs?
I remind myself the appointment is a coup for a civilian,
a coup for a woman.

When asked for my input on the mobile fire command centre,
I suggest a custom, adjustable, modular set-up.
The fire chief wants to go with the same design as last time,
a captain's chair and a mahogany roll-top in a cube van.
But he used to bang his head on the console
and there was no room for Logistics to install the plasma screen.
The underlings have their usual amnesia.

I argue for prevention.
Once built, it's complex to retrofit millwork,
expensive to rewire,
tricky, if not impossible, to change.

TRANSPORTATION DEPARTMENT, CITY OF TORONTO

With a three-point stance, the woman climbs the equipment,
measures clearances and step heights, observes the visual field,
while the men kick the massive tires,
ask about payload, huddle to tell jokes, linger.

Later the men will pull the manual choke
for diesel to flow.
Peering out of the cockpit,
they will depart, sweep away the woman's concern for safety,
seek frontiers beyond familiar streets.

The old man is her only ally.

He's seen too many accidents,
felt the blunt controls against his spleen
as the machine jerks to a stop,
witnessed an auger puncturing a hamstring.
He teaches her how to manipulate controls,
the snow load capacity of the plow;
he agrees that the steps are too high for easy egress,
suggests caution when broaching the idea.
"The men will drive it against a curb
just to prove you wrong," he says.
"Get them to buy in. Start with the gimp who is well-liked.
They'll pity him and not lose face."

She climbs the new step,
takes the controls, operates the bucket
to break new ground, discovers the same muck and rock.
With her new tool, she can break it down.

The tungsten lights shone on Gunther's crewcut,
reflected off the swastika on the inside of his red toolbox.
At seven a.m. he got out his German tools
to begin his millwright duties,
repaired punch presses and conveyers
operated by brown people with university degrees.
The punch press jammed after a crush injury
to Nadu's hand, or was it Vikram's?

After lunch (when Gunther sat
with the tradesmen and owners),
he was sent to fix the press
so the unskilled workers could stamp out more metal
for tamping machines and power trowels.

All day that toolbox stayed open.

SCRAPE

Mohammed kneels towards Mecca several times a shift.
A small mercy he's deaf,
though any fool can tell from the crew's twisted faces
that they're being cruel.

His crew calls him Mo.
They pick up white trash—not that kind—
appliances left at the curb.
In winter, they shovel snow.

Body broken from hard labour and hopelessness,
he rests in the truck cab
while his workmates heft old toilets onto the back.
They poke him awake with their shovels,
stop just short of a beating.

Now assigned to scrape posters from poles,
he walks ten miles through Parkdale in silence.

I'm called in to judge if his new job is suitable.
He removes his shoes,
rubs aching feet, points to blue toes.
Through the interpreter he says, "Tattered shoulder,"
says that he wants to drive a truck.
The supervisor insists, "It would be a promotion, it's out of the question."

He spits at Mo's refusal
to scrape detritus from the papal route—
overtime for the Pope's visit.
I prohibit extra hours even for Allah.
I tell him to assign one of his able Catholic boys.

I suggest insoles for his work boots, work below shoulder-level.
With that he is cleared to go.
Poster scraping is better
than his supervisor's next crusade—
Mo relegated to security, misfit on nightshift,
wooden benches in the lunchroom.
The wretched guard each other, forbidden to read,
random phone checks,
stench of abattoir across the equipment yard,
until they beg to return to day shifts.

Months later, he rests against a half-marred pole,
flags me down, gestures with deaf grunts and signs
that it's not working out,
points at failing body parts, grimaces.
Without the interpreter, all I manage is a nod.
He falls silent. His daughter leaves me a message—
"There is no dignity in my father's job. He is unhappy."
I call her back and say, "We don't consider dignity."

Too diffuse, his pain,
the system won't resolve his exile.
We must pinpoint the exact nature of discontent,
a diagnosis with known treatment.

Even I, who wince at the crew's attitude,
who wept for Muslims after 9/11,
am grateful he doesn't have sons
to send off to a radical mosque,
his daughter well-adjusted.
I'm ashamed.
This is what we're up against.

BLIND SPOT

The men and I sit around the table.
As the safety rep, I offer my dissent
on the purchase of street sweepers
due to poor sightlines for the driver.
The sales guy appeals to his pals,
accuses me of sleeping with the competitor,
while the men look on.
Later, when the deal is done,
outside, where we belong,
the chief mechanic whispers,
"Children in other cities have died
because the design obstructs the operators' vision,"
but he won't say this out loud because he's brown.

A BODY IS SEDUCED BY DAMAGES

A body is seduced by damages.
Swamp of bad blood, pump of glue,
it wants to wear a dress of bandages
and lose the human teeth and hair it grew.

> *from "Tendencies" by Heather McHugh*

His first time shocked,
fingertip glanced by a grinder,
distal knuckle ground down to nub,
attended to, swathed in white cloth,
sterile unlike anything else in a life.
Meanwhile, the messy bits lounge—
muffin-top gut, grubby nails,
sun-scarred ears, diffuse mind.
A body is seduced by damages.

That second time, the other hand,
a lacerated palm, surgical.
It's all the other labourers talked about:
easier to focus on the broken bits.
A small pension for each impairment,
"functional award," they call it.
Next a foot seduced by rock,
crushed, and the healers cleaned it up,
debrided then pinned back together, removed
swamp of bad blood, pump of glue.

The attention of experts: efficacy and kindness
pinpointed the site of trauma
and he wanted more.
A frayed shoulder
from a "heroic" exertion with a come-along.
Torn rotator cuff and a sling,
then chronic pain,
and he no longer feels like himself.
The body is something else, a tattered cross-dresser;
it wants to wear bandages.

Pensioned off.
They say it's cheaper to
keep him at home than risk
other amputations, internal injuries.

Body ambles, a disfigured ghost
on Crown land, scarred by old mine
tailings and rusted aerial trams.
All that's left to do, mercifully non-surgical,
is distinguish self from damage,
and lose the hair and human teeth it grew.

ASSISTED

Kathryn sits strapped and
reclined in her quadriplegic chair.
Beneath her power suit, her skin supple
from hands-on care, her fingers
limp, voice unreliable.
She settled on an assistive device, the mouth pointer,
to practice law.

Atop her desk a paper she's authored,
"Assisted Suicide."

When her head control is lost,
she will turn to a laser pointer controlled by eye movement.
Beyond that, there are no viable options.

THE ADAPTABLE SHALL INHERIT THE EARTH

The green bins were designed so the compost slop
could easily slide out:
slight camber, a lip
for the collector to grasp at hip height
and lift.

Curbside pickup of compost
had its detractors—
penny-pinching councillors,
avid gardeners who wouldn't part with rich "waste."
Raccoons first among them.

How to design a latch
to outsmart raccoons,
but easy enough for old ladies'
arthritic hands?

We tested latches with a force gauge,
scratched our heads. How many
highly paid professionals
does it take to outsmart a four-legged bandit?
We didn't learn raccoons' grip strength in school.
We settled on a combination of tricky and strong.

Three years later, to no avail,
bricks piled on bins from the Humber to the Rouge.
Homeowners resort to sophisticated bungee cords
to supplement the latch
that the raccoons have learned to break through.
We loathe their adaptation,

our cameras trained to catch their method.
Decent design no match for the thieves
knocking over the bins until their latches are breeched.
They feast,

waddle through city alleys,
swaying bellies. They've adapted well.
Pass on their wisdom to offspring:
Garbage collection is on Tuesday.

> *We took the expressway then turned left and had to*
> *detour to get down to tower one. We took the Brooklyn, no*
> *wait that's over on Flatbush, we took the Manhattan.*

Vigiles, first firemen,
wait outside while Marcus Crassus, the richest man in the Roman empire,
negotiates a price.
Otherwise the dwelling burns—
the original fire sale, before Christ.

> *All of the rigs now and the EMS and everything was*
> *on fire. We saw body parts falling. They were giving*
> *orders to take your rollups; you were going to fight the*
> *fire. A high-rise fire.*

Modeled on Crassus,
slaves of Augustus served Rome:
night watch, police force
bucket brigade.

> *The sound was so immense, we stopped the rig. We*
> *never stop the rig on the way to a run. The stairway*
> *was quite orderly: civilians coming down one side, fire*
> *department was headed up the other side.*

Through Victorian streets
fire companies raced in their felt top hats
with crude hand pumps and leather hoses—
cash reward for first on scene

You couldn't even talk; you had so much debris in your
mouth. He had a towel and he said we'll share and we'll
start breathing. There were like three of us on this towel.

In those days the *old guys* soaked their beards in water
for a breathing filter before they entered—
self-contained breathing apparatus evolves into
forty pounds of heavy air.

I call on the bullhorn, the radios, we're evacuating,
drop your tools, your masks, everything. Get out, get
out. We checked like five hydrants on South End.
They were all dead.

Iridescent bunker suit,
high-tech rubber boots,
standard-issue blue T-shirt,
six-pack abs beneath.
Fire-retardant hood,
traditional leather helmet (though lighter ones exist),
lest progress get in the way of tradition.
Battering rams,
searchlight hung from chest strap,
pike poles, axe,
no match for the collapse of 110 stories times two.

I remember forcing one beautiful mahogany door, thinking
wow, you can do some damage to this, you know. I had been
on Channel 3, the south tower. I think most of these guys
were dead, the guys that were on the same channel with me.

Dozens wait for orders in the concourse chaos.
The south tower's collapse:
news that hasn't yet spread
to overwhelmed radios.
Who knew the weight of two towers
could be inhaled by rescue squads
and ladder companies on scene?

> *I grabbed ahold of him, just stay with us now, because*
> *he was extremely lucky, he made it out twice and he*
> *was very shook up so I wanted to keep an eye on him.*
> *I encountered a jet engine somewhere on Church Street*
> *and decided this was not good and headed up*
> *Broadway.*

Trained to run into burning buildings,
this time, those who could, ran away and lived.
And with so few to find, the heroes still left would be unoccupied.
This was not a fire.

> *I heard the roof man from Ladder Four give a Mayday.*
> *Every time a body jumped, you just heard this thump, thump.*

Tragedy breaches every surface.
More firefighters suffer
sarcoidosis
respiratory ailments
PTSD
rare cancers.
Some retire early, some still jump into harm's way,
haunted by what they did or didn't do.
Their bunker suits can never be washed clean.

*There was a federal cop there who wouldn't let us up
the stairs; we went up the stairs anyway. I was in the
building when it came down. As far as I know, there
were eleven survivors out of both buildings. I'm
one of them. We were trapped four hours.*

Triumph and tragedy distill
to legend in the firehouse.
In the off-hours they tell these stories,
reinforce tradition, imbed glory.

Three hundred and forty-three firefighters dead.

*We stopped at the corner of Trinity and Liberty. It
was total darkness. We were there, we had no boss
and we just kind of wandered around aimlessly,
thinking, what can we do?*

The body count mounts through history.
Vigiles stand on watch.
For ages.
In the ruins.

*Finally I walked away hours later. Time
didn't really mean a whole lot.*

MEMORIAL
(reflection on For The Time Being *by Annie Dillard)*

Ground zero.
Water falls on black walls,
trickles, glistens.
Only their names remain;
solemn beauty attempts to assuage loss.

Shocking rearrangement of matter:
what was concrete, steel, human
is ash, dust.

Rush to commemorate
them. It.
Lest we sit in the wreckage,
hard to reconcile vulnerability.

If left, it would take seven centuries
to fill in the hole with debris:
dust, skin, sand, hair.
Now that's a memorial.

Fever of Gratitude

WAWA BOUND

Wawa must mean hope
in a language unknown to me.
The only sign: Wawa 110 km,
a beacon in my endless ascent and descent,
traversing a severe winter, an uncertain spring
in this dangerous season between solid and liquid,
past iced-over bays, jagged granite and spindly white pines,
infinite road that keeps a distance from the vast inland sea.

The sea reminds mountains that they are bound;
its immensity both buoys and diminishes me,
the sky but a mirror for its icy blue infinity.
Superior.

Is it gravity or the sea that grinds down the granite vertebrae
of these ancient mountains,
until they are decomposing bone chips
scattered along the battered beach?

I used to think signs told us nothing
of the destination or the journey
but tonight as the sun fades, the only posts
are the lengthening shadows of spruce on this long stretch of road.
Absence whispers through the trees.
Even settlers knew enough to leave this land alone.

LIMP

A fender-bender with a Lexus.
The other driver frowned
as he watched her limp towards her trunk.
Taking her for a faker,
he waited impatiently
while she retrieved her purse for the insurance slip.
His frown slid into something else when he saw a leg in the trunk.
He stalled and called the police discreetly from his car;
she smirked as two officers arrived followed by two more.
They'd called for backup.
Their hands on their guns as they issued rapid-fire instructions
but she willingly popped her trunk.
The car jack and spare tire bookended her extra prosthetic,
which had rolled out of its blanket at impact.
The other driver was huffy,
saying, "How was I to know it was a fake leg?" and
"There are a lot of freaks around these days."
The police stood at a distance, their arms limp at their sides,
apologized for the inconvenience
or her missing leg, she can't be sure which.

WOMEN AT FORTY
(after Donald Justice)

Women at forty
have learned to open loudly
the doors to shut rooms.
Having resolved the question of children
either way,
they are renewed,
having learned to sail after being refused
entry to the ship's engine room.
Something fills them, sails billowing,
a long beam reach.

Now, when a forty-year-old enters a room,
her sheets snap firm.
Harvesting the wind,
no filth of diesel,
no need.
Her house. Her door.

NOT DISTRACTED BY GRAVITY

I release the clasp of your belt:
mouth on mouth
we fumble until our layers fall
in a heap to the ground.

Weightless,
not distracted by gravity,
without the pull of the moon or our mothers,
we don't look back at the earth, only at each other.
In heaven there is no tongue so limited as English,
so lucid it doesn't entangle,
words don't form and diminish.
The ancient language trembles lips
as our bodies surrender in silence.

The divine tumbles away in a last kiss;
the thump of the neighbour's fist on a common wall
crashes us back to earth,
ill-equipped as we are with nakedness and truth
when the world demands armour and wit.

The word *buckle* forms on my lips as I dress.
Glorious silver buckle.
The pungent sting of curry wafts up from the flat below.
The family will leave some at our door
and we, in turn,
will offer luscious, bleeding strawberries from our garden.

THE PERILS OF CARTOGRAPHY

This sheet of our world
omits rocks and hills.
The town appears as a grid interrupted,
squiggly roads fade away into something unknown—
a park, a badland, or a granite cliff at the base of a mountain.

The foreign mapmaker, from afar, charts our territory,
but we've no use for symbols with life so close at hand.
We know which way is north without the compass rose.

The map doesn't show the patient stonework at our front gate,
or the neighbour's languid tulips at midday.
The rhythm of children skipping after supper,
or the rolling thunder of skateboarders.
It doesn't show the way the dense conifers compost the noise of town
or the dappled sunlight through the apple tree.
It's oblivious to the house shading the deck
from the scorch of the afternoon,
the ever-moderate temperature of the kitchen,
rooted too far in the earth to be affected by air.
It doesn't show white plum blossoms, dancing wildly to avoid May hail
or the way the sky turns purple while
beyond the mountains, the sun burns itself out for another day.

The toiling cartographer is unaware that
the glacier-fed lake transforms us
when we plunge in,
and then narrows itself into a river
off the edge of our porch. The river—
that slow-moving deep animal that carries our dreams and
deposits them downstream
for us to collect on an autumn paddle some years later.

The street grid abruptly stops on the map,
giving no hint of mountains except to the cartographer
who comprehends the magnitude of natural barriers
like a land-locked body understands diving in water.

FEVER OF GRATITUDE

Deep contemplation, Bach's cello suites usher in morning light
as sun appears over the green mountain
and slender thermometers of grass
shed the glistening mercury of night:
elusive quicksilver, poured from the sky, dances in starlight
and disappears each morning into damp September earth.

By day the grasses grow redder
in a fever of gratitude
for the season, for transition,
in this frenzy of free fall, autumn.
We have been busy tracing root systems
back to the source, trusting our substance,
standing up in the wind but learning to bend.

I want us to rest like quiet blades of grass
in each other's arms, alive and steaming.

LOCAL COMMUTE

The only airline that flies here
offers an open-ended commuter pass.
If I still worked away, I'd consider the deal.

Instead I'm mulling over sprouted quinoa bread versus
quinoa salad, but different this time, red.
I'm wondering what's worse: dog pee or pesticides
on the dandelion greens that I picked with my kids.

Good deal or not, the flight pass offer goes in the junk box.
Gone, too, are the notices of protest for a pipeline up north.
This year the garden wants its pound of flesh, but no,
it doesn't abide metaphor.
Earth demands worm casings and nitrogen, tug of shovel.

Already I'm imagining cleaving the suckers from the beefsteaks,
bartering garlic for plums,
as seeds settle beneath horse shit and straw
and contrails vaporize as fast as they appear.

RASPBERRY PANCAKES

A Tuesday morning and I'm mixing high-fibre batter in a bowl,
dropping the delicate, full-lipped raspberries in, one by one.
The berries sizzle with the heat of the grill
and the sweet smell demotes the everyday aroma of coffee.
I know the pancakes will make me late,
but the alternative is not okay on this workday,
during which I will calmly and routinely make entitlement decisions.
Another breakfast of toast would kill me.

Flapjack, griddlecake, pancake,
not a cake
but a misshapen, bubbling disc
that finds its own edges.
God is on the griddle and the devil too.
It's the Virgin Mary, and now a heart
pink and brown
like a sunburned gringo.
Outside the sun's not yet up,
but makes its way slowly over the mountains.

Swimming in oil, the lustrous first,
even so, holds the fluffy promise of more
and I believe.
Yogurt dollop
atop a lake of maple syrup
renders them divine.
These unlikely stars
are finicky and beyond knowing.

SOLSTICES

Artificial light, busyness,
our urgency and ignorance.
We hear quiet tick-tock
muffled by the whir of small appliances.
Unplugged.
Retreat into the beautiful hours of dark
with only one foot-candle to light our way.
Awaken, then work and play late into June's light.
These two days a year we toy with harmony,
so much fluorescence to overcome.

BEAUTY CAST OFF IN ADVANCING AUTUMN

You see, the bears inhabited their yard,
a sit-in until the fat, sweet globes of apples ripen
on the ancient, twisted trees.
They stalked the orchard at dawn
and, once the husband was gone, peered
in the windows at mother and baby.

Now the orchard is a field
in the shadows of two trees: a lone plum and a solitary pear.
But there is only so much one can let go of.
The husband unwilling to part with the pear's perfect female form,
and the wife would not forgo the succulence of plums.

Ghosts of the ungrown apples may inhabit the ripening fruit.
A hint of tart in the pear, a crunch in the plum.
Even sweeter in the apples' absence, they will ripen,
while rooted trunks watch on, abandoned.
The bears will groan at the harvest moon,
whose light shines a clear path through the meadow.

Spirits, with the apples' ripe aroma, breeze through
and the last bear lingers,
her nose up, snorting at the musky fragrance
in the near-empty orchard at dawn.

BRIEF CEREMONY

Light shimmers through December dawn like a ghost into a room.
Not so dormant, a sentry of trees skirts an open field.
At midday, limbs trickle their winter stripes onto frozen ground,
afternoon brings brief ceremony, a stiff dance
in solemn imitation of fluttering leaves—
a skeletal sway mocking summer's ruckus.
Even twigs are anchored firm in their fractal black span,
determined to escape a leaf's fate,
as dusk inks through the winter sky.

Stoic trees absorb their weight in darkness,
retreat—
ushering in another night.

The tree knows retreat, living bark against the wind,
growing inwards, becoming xylem and pithy centre.
The quiet, strong heartwood.

ENOUGH

The fully open lily with its sex exposed,
pink to the world,
stamen erect,
languid petals,
its strong stem
leaning towards the sun,
or the light, for there is no sun
facing the north mountains in winter.
Still, it is enough.
I sit here watching
un-shamed pistils float.

SKUNK CABBAGE

Skunk cabbage erupts in the perimeter woods,
liminal.
Skunk and cabbage.
Neither.

Bright yellow spathes,
tightly wrapped romaine
unfurl their smell,
displeasing us.

Swamp lanterns light up a dim day
on this path between manicured woods and granite walls.
First blooms in spring—nourishment for bears,
preserving wrap for salmon,
reluctant food in times of famine.

I wasn't thinking of quitting my job on this morning walk,
but the plant has convinced me
the logic of paycheque and pension is overrated.
Art, too, can be this brash, nonsensical—
plant that smells like an animal and is named for food.

Untamed, I will write, spathed in red, diaphanous spirit
that neither protects nor explains.
Not animal nor plant.

LAST LAKE SWIM OF THE YEAR

Lithe body, accustomed shore.
Discarded clothes, peak of day,
empty beach, aching sky.

Determined to do more than dip,
you linger, inhale the musk
of October rot.
The larches golden, your toes numb,
by now you're certain
it's the last swim.

Your body knows the ritual—
tussles with sadness
and laughter accumulated
from all the other swims.

Skin tingling, organs awake,
you wade in slow
like it's the heat of July,
like you have all the time in the world.

Plunge beyond surface warmth,
engulfed in alpine-
lake cold:
there is nothing next.

AT THIS HOUR
for Betty Daniel, 90.

Long twilight,
almost unnoticed,
until the glacier and the endless day you took for granted,
are gone—
your hand a silhouette.

There is relief in darkness:
sag and wrinkles invisible,
expectations of the day evaporate,
like low-hung clouds
giving way to a half-moon belly dancing on water,
not to be compared to the light of afternoon.

There are moments of sparkle in the darkness—
the firefly, the flame,
that also bring warmth,
mingled with memories
of your full life.

At this hour, you risk delight.

ACKNOWLEDGEMENTS

For their support and keen attention I would like to acknowledge my poetry group, Linda Crosfield, Bobbie Ogletree and Susan Andrews Grace. Susan deserves a special thanks for seeing these poems as a whole before I could, and for editing an early version of the manuscript. I would like to acknowledge my parents, Alan and Pat Byers, and my grandmother, Blanche Byers, for their grit and unconditional love. Thank you to Rhea Tregebov, Cleopatra Mathis and James Kelway for their early guidance. Thank you to Christopher Broadhurst, Kate Clark, Sharon Larade, Priscilla McLellan, Valerie Stetson, Pat Rayman and Tom Wayman. Thank you to Nelson, BC, for embracing and nurturing my creative self.

Thank you also to editors of the following publications in which earlier versions of these poems appeared: the *Antigonish Review, Descant, Grain,* the *Canadian Journal of Hockey Literature, Rattle,* the *New Orphic Review, Horsefly, Ars Medica, Seasonings* and *Our Times.*

Jane Byers lives with her wife and two children in Nelson, British Columbia. She writes about human resilience in the context of raising children, lesbian and gay issues, sexism, local geography and health and safety in the workplace. She spent many years working for the City of Toronto in corporate health and safety and now works at WorkSafeBC where she continues to facilitate resilience in injured workers. She has had poems, essays and short fiction published in a variety of books and literary magazines in Canada, the US, and the UK, including *Grain, Rattle, Descant,* the *Antigonish Review,* the *Canadian Journal of Hockey Literature* and *Our Times.* She is a three-time winner of the Nelson and District Poetry Competition.